Welcome, Baby

Before You Were Born

Before you were conceived I wanted you.
Before you were born I loved you...
This is the miracle of life.

MAUREEN HAWKINS

Before you were born...

Why having you felt important:

Great Expectations

Finding out you were coming was: ______________________________

____

____

____

____

____

The first signs that you were on the way were: ______________________________

____

____

____

____

____

The first people to know about you were:

How your news was celebrated:

The future starts today...

POPE JOHN PAUL II

Shared joy
is double
joy...

SWEDISH PROVERB

Showered with Love

The first party for you was:

It was held on:

And it was hosted by:

The most surprising gift was:

The best piece of advice was:

Counting the Days

Waiting for you was:

You were expected to come on:

PLACE SONOGRAM HERE

Family... where life begins
and love never ends.

UNKNOWN

The Day You Were Born

Seeing you for the first time was: ______________________________

____

____

____

____

____

____

____

____

____

____

____

____

____

____

You were born on ____________ *at* ____________ *in the city of* ____________

You weighed ____________ *and measured* ____________

Family is not an important thing, it's everything.

MICHAEL J. FOX

PLACE PHOTO HERE

Welcome to the World

*Small child—once you were a hope,
a dream. Now you are reality. Changing all
that is to come. So small. A flick of star stuff.
A mind to touch the edges of the universe.
A love to hold our hearts forever.*

CHARLOTTE GRAY

The Story of Your Birth

...memory is a way of holding onto the things you love, the things you are, the things you never want to lose.

THE WONDER YEARS, 1988

All Your Visitors

With every newborn baby, a little sun rises.

IRMGARD ERATH

When you name your baby, it's a time of dreaming.

LAURA WATTENBERG

Another Name for Love

Your name was chosen because:

Other names considered were:

Here are some nicknames for you:

Your Little Fingers & Toes

BABY'S HANDPRINTS

BABY'S FOOTPRINTS

No one understands how someone so little can so change their world—until they hold their baby in their arms.

PAM BROWN

The World Awaits You

The World When You Were Born

President's name:

Big items in the news:

Latest inventions:

Popular songs:

TV shows:

Movies:

The Price of a...

While we try to teach our children all about life,
our children teach us what life is all about.

ANGELA SCHWINDT

A Brand-New Dream, A Brand-New World

A possibility was born the day you were born and it will live as long as you live.

MARCUS SOLERO

Welcome Home

...what joy is welcomed like a new-born child?

CAROLINE NORTON

Your first day home was: ____________

The weather that day: ____________

You were dressed in: ____________

Some of your first visitors at home were: ____________

Memories of that day: ____________

Your First Room

Here's what your room is like:

...home is where your favorite memories are.

PIETER-DIRK UYS

And these are your first books:

Some of your favorite toys:

Some special touches:

Getting to Know You

Your First Two Weeks

A day with you is: ______________________________

____

You wake up: ______________________________

You're very active when: ______________________________

____

____

You seem to like it when: ______________________________

____

____

Some memorable moments: ______________________________

____

____

____

____

...do not hurry
the journey
at all.

CONSTANTINE P. CAVAFY

...there are only two lasting bequests we can hope to give our children. One of these... is roots, the other, wings.

HODDING CARTER

Our Family Tree

A Letter to You

Dear ____________________,

Love, ____________

...all that is worth cherishing in this world begins in the heart...

SUZANNE CHAZIN

First Milestones and Little Miracles

From small beginnings come great things.

PROVERB

Smiles & Giggles

The first time you smiled:

And the first time you laughed:

Some things that always make you smile and giggle are:

Children are a handful sometimes, a heart-full all the time.

UNKNOWN

Your First Haircut

Your first haircut was on: ______________________

It was at: ______________________

____

Here's how it went: ______________________

____

____

____

____

____

____

____

____

I can still remember rocking
them to sleep on my lap
in the middle of the night,
to soothe them back to sleep
after a stomach ache or
a bad dream, the songs
I would make up...

BETTY FRIEDAN

Watching You Grow

First & Second Months

Every child begins the world again...

HENRY DAVID THOREAU

You're changing: ______________________________

____

____

____

And now you can: ______________________________

____

____

You like: ______________________________

____

____

Favorite memories: ______________________________

____

____

____

____

____

Now you're __________ *inches and* __________ *pounds*

DATE: ______________

Watching You Grow

Third & Fourth Months

I actually remember feeling delight, at two o'clock in the morning, when the baby woke for his feed, because I so longed to have another look at him.

MARGARET DRABBLE

You're changing: ____________________

____

____

____

And now you can: ____________________

____

____

You like: ____________________

____

____

Favorite memories: ____________________

____

____

____

____

____

Now you're __________ *inches and* __________ *pounds*

DATE: ____________

Watching You Grow

Fifth & Sixth Months

Babies touch the world with love.

UNKNOWN

You're changing: ______________________________

____

____

____

And now you can: ______________________________

____

____

You like: ______________________________

____

____

Favorite memories: ______________________________

____

____

____

____

____

Now you're ____________ *inches and* ____________ *pounds*

DATE: ____________

Watching You Grow

Seventh & Eighth Months

...joy is everywhere...

RABINDRANATH TAGORE

You're changing: ______________________

____

____

____

And now you can: ______________________

____

____

You like: ______________________

____

____

Favorite memories: ______________________

____

____

____

____

____

Now you're __________ *inches and* __________ *pounds*

DATE: ______________

Watching You Grow

Ninth & Tenth Months

Children reinvent your world for you.

SUSAN SARANDON

You're changing: ______

And now you can: ______

You like: ______

Favorite memories: ______

Now you're ______ *inches and* ______ *pounds*

DATE: ______

Watching You Grow

Eleventh & Twelfth Months

Some things don't last forever, but some things do.

SARAH DESSEN

You're changing: ______________________________

____

____

____

And now you can: ______________________________

____

____

You like: ______________________________

____

____

Favorite memories: ______________________________

____

____

____

____

____

Now you're ____________ *inches and* ____________ *pounds*

DATE: ____________

Your First Birthday

Here's how you celebrated your first birthday: ______

You wore: ______

You received well-wishes on your special day from:

PLACE PHOTO HERE

Expect the most wonderful things to happen...

EILEEN CADDY

Little You

It's so wonderful watching you:

You seem fascinated by:

Think... of the world you carry within you.

RAINER MARIA RILKE

Some of your favorite things are:

And the people you're happy to see are:

A New Life with You

Your arrival has meant some big changes, including:

A baby will make love stronger, days shorter, nights longer, bankroll smaller, home happier, clothes shabbier, the past forgotten, and the future worth living for.

UNKNOWN

*Love has nothing
to do with what you
are expecting to get–
only with what you
are expecting to give–
which is everything.*

KATHARINE HEPBURN

A Future So Bright

In your first year, we've started some new traditions:

And shared special moments together, like:

Some hopes for the year to come include:

COMPENDIUM®
live inspired

Written and Compiled by: Dan Zadra and Amelia Riedler
Illustrated by: Clare Therese Gray
Designed by: Jessica Phoenix
Edited by: Miriam Hathaway

ISBN: 978-1-957891-49-1

1st printing. Printed in China with soy inks on FSC®-Mix certified paper.

Create meaningful moments with gifts that inspire.

CONNECT WITH US
live-inspired.com | sayhello@compendiuminc.com

@compendiumliveinspired
#compendiumliveinspired